Amazing of the Sea

Danny Pearson

Badger Publishing Limited
Oldmedow Road,
Hardwick Industrial Estate,
King's Lynn PE30 4JJ
Telephone: 01438 791037

www.badgerlearning.co.uk

4 6 8 10 9 7 5 3

Amazing Animals of the Sea ISBN 978-1-78147- 827-1

Text © Danny Pearson 2014
Complete work © Badger Publishing Limited 2014

All rights reserved. No part of this publication may be reproduced, stored in any form or by any means mechanical, electronic, recording or otherwise without the prior permission of the publisher.

The right of Danny Pearson to be identified as author of this work has been asserted by him in accordance with the Copyright, Designs and Patents Act 1988.

Publisher: Susan Ross
Senior Editor: Danny Pearson
Publishing Assistant: Claire Morgan
Designer: Fiona Grant
Series Consultant: Dee Reid

Photos: Cover image: © Rich Carey/iStock
Page 4: Jurgen Freund/Nature Picture/REX
Page 5: Reinhard Dirscherl/Robert Harding
Page 6: Image Broker/REX
Page 7: Image Broker/REX, James Forte/National Geographic/Robert Harding
Page 12: Bill Curtsinger/National Geographic/Getty Images
Page 13: Jeff Rotman/Nature Picture L/REX
Page 14: © Ifremer/A. Fifis/Courtesy M. Segonzac (MNHN)/Press Association Images
Page 15: Phil Yeomans/REX
Page 17: Image Broker/REX
Page 18: Peter Oxford/Nature Picture/REX
Page 19: © Paul Fleet/Alamy
Page 20: Masa Ushioda/Robert Harding
Page 21: Michael Nolan/Robert Harding
Page 22: Masa Ushioda/Robert Harding
Page 23: Christopher Swann/Specialist/REX
Page 24: Jonas Liebschner/REX
Page 25: Paul Nicklen/National Geographic/Getty Images
Page 27: Brian J Skerry/National Geographic/Getty Images
Page 29: Stephen Wong/SplashdownDirec/REX
Page 30: Ross Armstrong/age fotostock/Robert Harding

Attempts to contact all copyright holders have been made.
If any omitted would care to contact Badger Learning, we will be happy to make appropriate arrangements.

Contents

1.	Cool creatures under the sea	5
2.	Scary fish	9
3.	Crazy crabs	14
4.	Giants of the sea	19
5.	More wonders of the sea	24
	Questions	31
	Index	32

Vocabulary

algae   creature
Arctic   oceans
coconut   predators
coral   prey

1. Cool creatures under the sea

Some amazing animals live in the seas and oceans.

Sea squirt

The sea squirt is an amazing animal.

It finds a rock to live on. Then it stays there for the rest of its life. When it is hungry it eats its own brain!

Sea cucumber

The sea cucumber is an amazing creature. It lives on the sea bed. If it gets hurt it can grow a new part of its body.

Leafy sea dragon

The leafy sea dragon is a type of seahorse. It has small fins on its back to help it move. Bigger animals don't eat it because they think it is seaweed!

Blobfish

This is a blobfish.

Why do you think it is called that?

WOW! facts

More than 70% of the world is covered with water.

2. Scary fish

Deep sea hatchetfish

The deep sea hatchetfish is a very scary-looking animal.

It lives at the bottom of the sea.

The deep sea hatchetfish can make its own light. This light helps hide it from bigger animals.

Barreleye fish

Barreleye fish have amazing eyes. You can see right inside them!

Their eyes look straight up to see food above them.

Pacu fish

The Pacu is a fish with amazing teeth.

Do you think they look like human teeth?

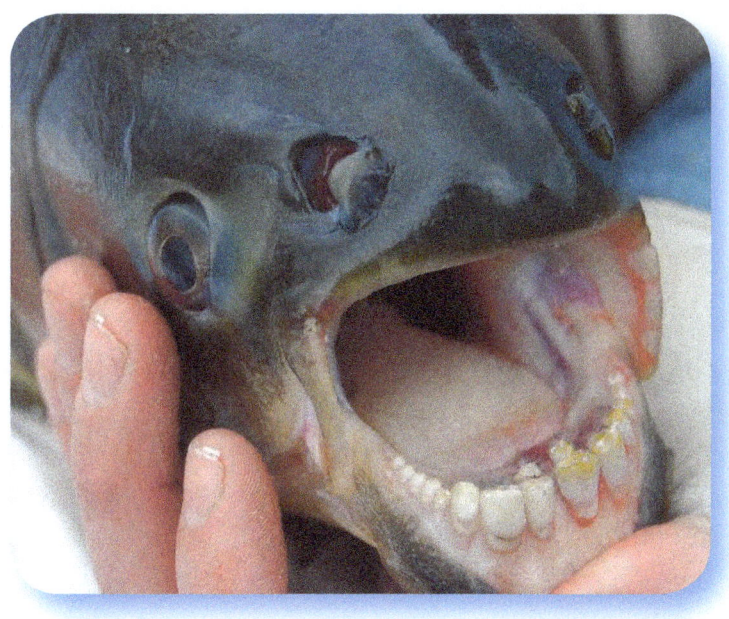

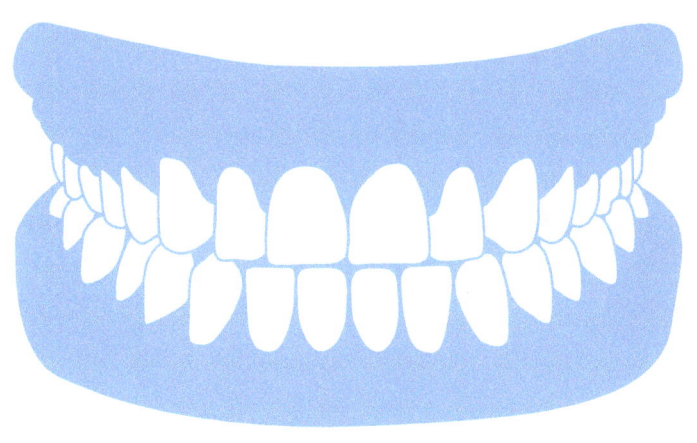

Cookiecutter shark

The cookiecutter shark also has amazing teeth.

When it bites its prey it leaves round holes where its teeth have bitten.

WOW! facts
Cookiecutter sharks have been known to attack humans.

Parrot fish

The parrot fish has amazing colours on its body. It lives on coral reefs.

Why is it called the parrot fish?

Because it has a beak for a mouth. The beak helps it to eat algae from the hard coral.

3. Crazy crabs

Yeti crab

This is an amazing crab.

Why is it called the yeti crab?

Because it has long hair all over its legs and pincers. This special hair helps it to live in deep parts of the sea where the water is toxic.

Spider crab

The spider crab is amazing. It can grow to over three metres long.

It looks scary but it is a gentle creature and does not bite.

Red crab

Some people think crabs are scary.

Every year, millions of these red crabs crawl out of the sea onto Christmas Island.

Would you be scared if you saw a million red crabs?

Hermit crab

A hermit crab lives in a shell. As the crab grows, it gets too big for its shell, so it moves out to find a bigger shell.

Some hermit crabs do not find bigger shells. This hermit crab has made its home in a used shell.

Coconut crab

The coconut crab is one of the biggest crabs in the world. What would you do if you saw this crab crawling up your beach towel?

WOW! facts
Coconut crabs can grow up to one metre long.

4. Giants of the sea

Giant squid

Long ago, sailors thought the giant squid was a sea monster. The giant squid can grow to over 20 metres. It has ten long arms that it uses to attack other animals.

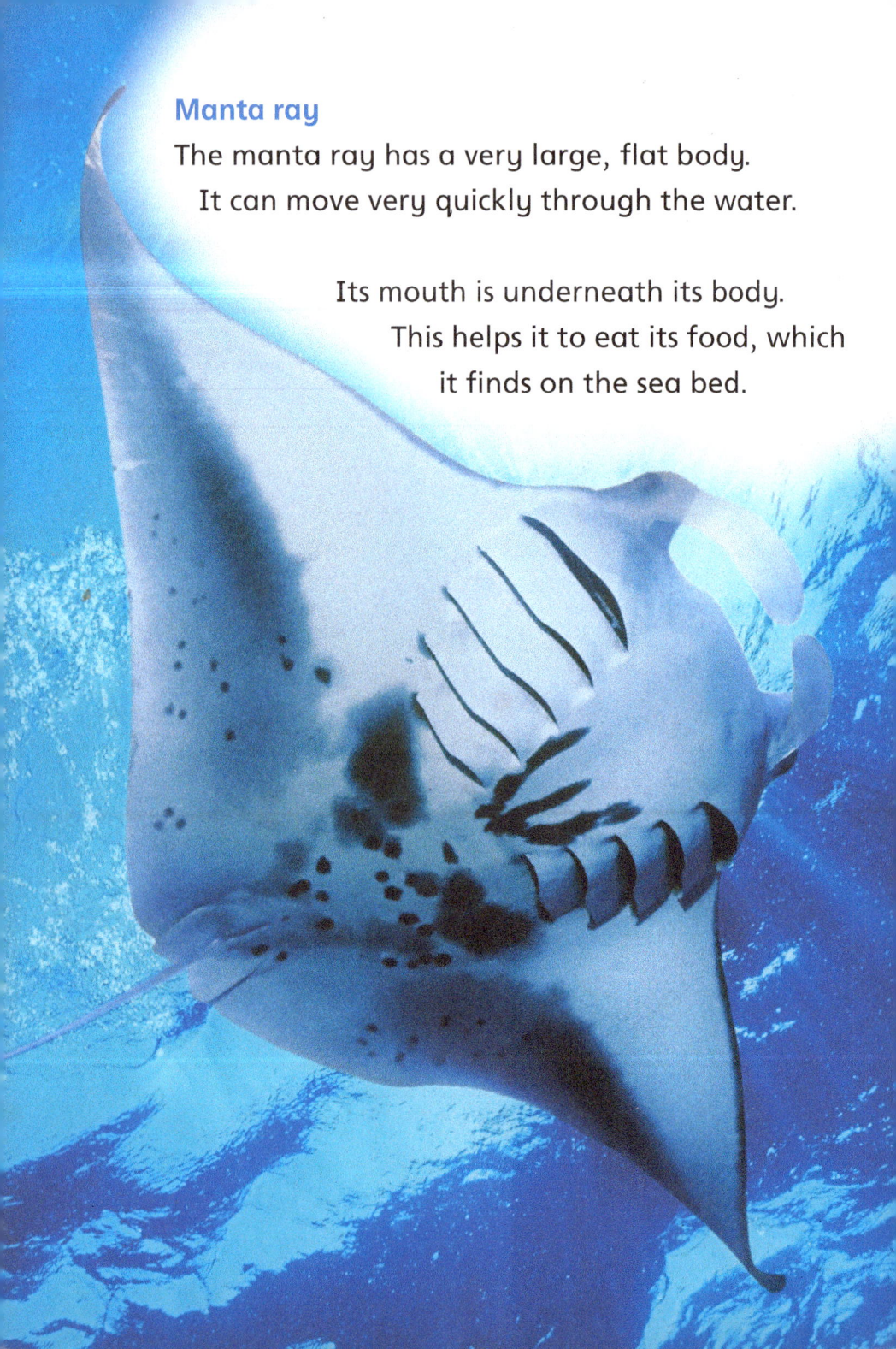

Manta ray

The manta ray has a very large, flat body.
It can move very quickly through the water.

Its mouth is underneath its body.
This helps it to eat its food, which
it finds on the sea bed.

Elephant seal

The elephant seal is very big and fat. It can weigh as much as two tonnes.

Elephant seals live in large groups. Male elephant seals like to fight. They don't smell too good either.

Ocean sunfish

The ocean sunfish is a real giant. It can grow to the size of a car!

Blue whale

The blue whale is the biggest animal in the world. It only eats tiny animals called krill, but it does eat four tonnes of them every day.

WOW! facts

Blue whales can grow up to 30 metres long and weigh up to 170 tonnes.

5. More wonders of the sea

Flying fish get their name because they jump out of the water. It looks like they are flying. They spread out their fins like wings to 'fly' away from bigger fish.

The narwhal lives in the cold waters of the Arctic. It has a very large horn on its head that is actually a giant tooth.

The vampire squid is a cross between a squid and an octopus.

It does not drink blood but it is a dark red colour and it has red eyes, which is why it is called the vampire squid.

The firefly squid makes its own light.

These squid meet up in large numbers. They put on the most amazing light shows.

When you first look at the fringehead fish it looks quite normal.

But look at what it looks like when it is under attack! It shows off its very scary mouth to scare away bigger fish.

A mimic octopus is a very clever animal.

It can change the shape of its body to scare off predators or to attract its food.

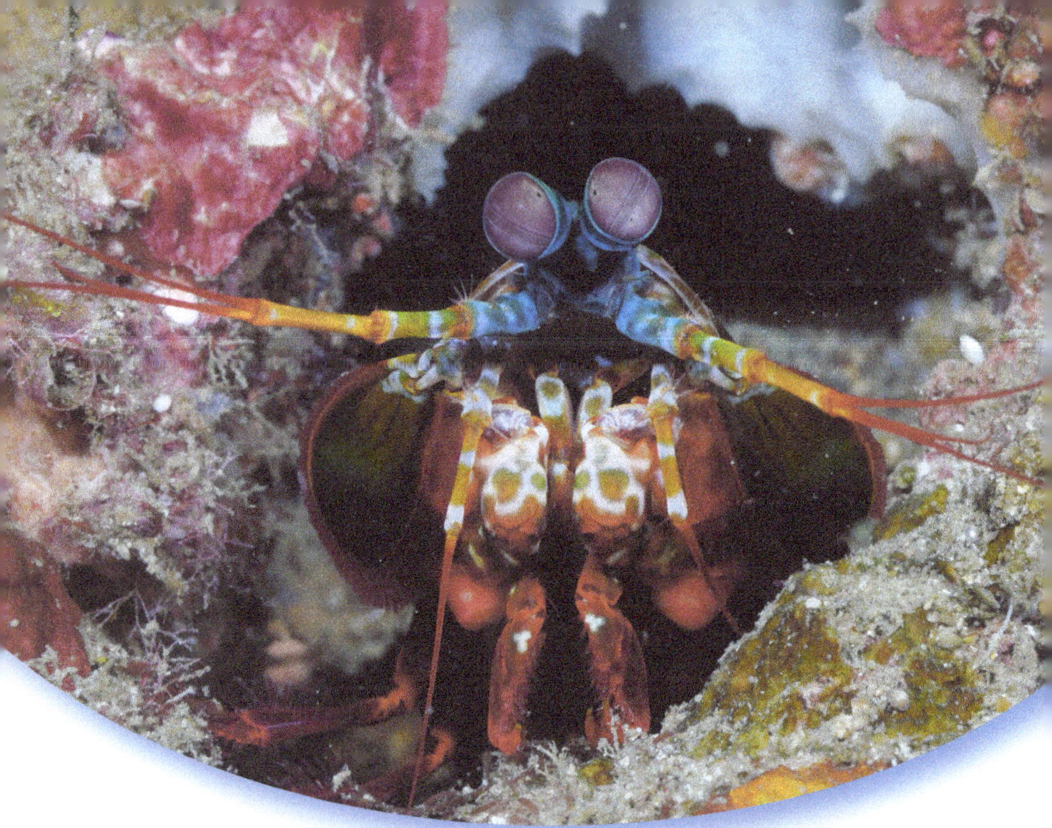

This is the peacock mantis shrimp. This shrimp only grows 3 to 18 centimetres long but it has the hardest punch on Earth. It knocks out its prey with its super hard punch.

WOW! facts

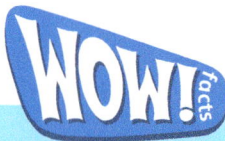

The peacock mantis shrimp's punch moves at the same speed as a bullet being fired from a gun. It is so fast, the water around it boils!

Questions

How much of the world is covered in water? *(page 8)*

Where does the deep sea hatchetfish live? *(page 9)*

What do parrot fish eat using their beaks? *(page 13)*

How big can a spider crab grow? *(page 15)*

Which island is visited by millions of red crabs every year? *(page 16)*

What does the blue whale eat? *(page 23)*

Index

barreleye fish 10
blobfish 8
blue whale 23
Christmas Island 16
coconut crab 18
cookiecutter shark 12
coral reefs 13
deep sea hatchetfish 9
elephant seal 21
firefly squid 27
flying fish 24
fringehead fish 28
giant squid 19
hermit crab 17
krill 23
leafy sea dragon 7
manta ray 20
mimic octopus 29
narwhal 25
ocean sunfish 22
pacu fish 11
parrot fish 13
peacock mantis shrimp 30
red crab 16
sea cucumber 7
sea squirt 6
spider crab 15
vampire squid 26
yeti crab 14